Presented to

Diss

S0-ANF-370

From

Mark, Dorothy, Elizabeth &
Rachel Date ___8-19-89___

Love Goes On Forever

BAKER BOOK HOUSE

Grand Rapids, Michigan 49516

Written and Illustrated by
Samuel J. Butcher

Design coordinator
William Biel

Published by Baker Book House
with permission of the
copyright owner

ISBN: 0-8010-0964-2

Printed in USA

To
Judy Markham
my forever friend

The gift of love is rare

but flows
in great abundance
when it's found.

Love wipes away our tears

and warms the heart;

Love understands

and heals,

it shelters
from the storm;

Love wings its way
above the circumstance

and goes beyond the sea
to touch a heart.

Love always
stands behind us

yet it goes before
to lead us into peace.

Though songs are sung

*and books written
about it*

love is an act
that means the most
when it is shared.

True love is given —
never earned

though sometimes
it is spent;

it never fails –
but reaches on,

for love is heaven-sent

Beloved,
let us love one another;
for love is of God ...

1 John 4:7